Effective Root Cause Analysis

Looking at control, responsibility, process improvement and making the whole activity more effective

Disclaimer:

The author of this book has tried to present the most accurate information to his knowledge at the time of writing. This book is intended for information purposes only. The author does not imply any results to those using this book, nor are they responsible for any results brought about by the usage of the information contained herein.

No part of this book may be reprinted, electronically transmitted or reproduced in any format without the express written permission of the author.

Contents

Introduction and "warning" 7
The issue(s) at hand 11
A recap on root cause problem solving approaches 17
The idea 33
The questions 43
Moving from decision into action 47
Stories 57
Opportunities 71
Conclusion 103
Reference and further reading 109
About Giles 111

Introduction and "warning"

Thanks for picking up this book.

Firstly, I hope that you enjoy it and find the ideas I share to be useful to you (both on a personal and a business level). If you are new to root cause problem solving or want to get a little more performance for your business, then I aim to share with you something valuable. You will certainly be able to make your business become more effective and more efficient. Root cause analysis is a superb approach to find out what is really going in your business and make some far reaching and permanent changes. In this book I will guide you through some of the best (and simplest) approaches to conducting root cause analyses.

Secondly, let me share with you a quick note about why this book might not be for everyone. There is a large focus in this book about personal responsibility. Carrying out a root cause analysis can be a momentous activity for a business; a real performance breakthrough can occur if you dig far enough into the reasoning and logic of how your business works. If you apply this to personal responsibility at the same time then you can achieve even more potent results. This might mean looking at some of your failings head on and making decisions about how you change your style / behaviour / approach going forward.

This book isn't solely to grumble about your shortcomings (we all have them!), but you have been warned. Also, this approach can be applied at every level of every organisation so, as I write this, I am hoping that you will be able to take out the positives from this extension to root cause analysis and make a real difference to both your personal effectiveness and your business' results.

Finally, let me acknowledge that 'stuff happens' and personal responsibility will only go so far. Levels of influence, ability and the strange way that the Universe works need to be factored in. It won't stop us from becoming more effective and achieving better results, but let's be realistic. Sometimes stuff happens and the root cause of that particular issue might be so far away from our ability to resolve it might seem pointless. But, our ability to respond will always be available to us and we can keep this point in mind as we progress through the following pages.

Enjoy the book. I have kept it as short as I possibly can to make it as accessible as possible. Take the ideas and bend them and shape them into a form that works for you. Most importantly, experiment with your own experiences and situations to apply the bits of this book that make the most sense to you.

Sit back, absorb and then go play!

Giles

The issue(s) at hand

So, why have I decided to write a book about root cause analysis and the need for greater levels of personal responsibility? The tools that I will share with you in this book can really make a difference to business performance. I really believe this. I am like a stuck record with my clients and for a very good reason. Root cause analysis can be transformational when focused in the right areas and when the attitude used to carry out the analyses is in the right place.

Let me talk you through what are, in my opinion, the issue(s) at hand with this topic. You should then understand exactly why I felt the need to write this book and what to expect further on.

We look at problems as if they are new

Businesses have lots of problems. Problems are there all the time and core problems may slowly change over time. Some problems are new but many of them are the same old issue re-surfacing in a different way (see the next point). As we tend to think of the problems as all being different, we then get paralysed with deciding where we want to start our investigations. The beauty of root cause analysis is that you can start anywhere, because the origins of the problem are often few. If you have read any of my other books you may well recall the manufacturing business I like to quote that had over one hundred and fifty post it notes on their office walls detailing all of their current woes. Once we carried out some effective root cause analysis (their previous approach was somewhat aggressive and didn't yield much in terms of results) it turned out there were only three things that they needed to focus on to make significant progress with their overall improvements. One hundred and fifty issues, three real issues.

In this book I'll share with you the same approach that I used with this business.

Shortcomings of root cause analysis

On many occasions, when I see root cause analysis being carried out (I'm going to use the shorthand of RCA going forward), I see it coming up short. The teams pull their ideas together and try to understand the cause and effect relationships that are going on around them. RCA isn't always the easiest thing to undertake if you're new to it and as soon as the team think they have gotten to a root cause their momentum slows. The team think that they have arrived at the root and are happy to put in place an action to resolve the situation once and for all. The only trouble is that many times they haven't arrived at the correct destination and they are still talking about symptoms that the business has. Without truly arriving at the root cause they will find that the symptoms will manifest as something else in due course. The corrective actions chosen will not deal with the underlying issue effectively.

Later in this book I have some simple questions that will help you to drive to a true root cause and turn the power of this process up a few notches!

RCA can take a long time...

Another grumble that I hear about using RCA is that it can take a long time to find out the answers that you need. In actual fact, whilst this could be the case when facts need to be gathered and data crunched, most other cases can be solved in a matter of minutes. Of course, this depends on how skilled you are at applying the tools, how open your colleagues are to having a conversation and how much data needs to be analysed. In my experience more business problems are resolved qualitatively rather than quantitatively and that's good news for you and your team.

Qualitative problems require exploration of ideas, standards and processes rather than hard data. As long as you have all of the right people around the table when you start a RCA exercise then you should find that the time is well spent and that you are not stuck in the middle of a time draining event.

This book will focus on the tools that are geared towards qualitative assessment. I will also push you past basic cause and effect relationships, to something more powerful.

Limited application

RCA is not applied to every opportunity that it could be. I often see it used when dealing with business non-conformities (as you would carry out when executing an ISO 9001 type quality management system), but application in other areas is patchy.

In this book I am going to encourage you to apply the tools far and wide and not stop with just production type problems, health and safety incidents and business non-conformities. As

I said just a moment ago, it doesn't really matter where you start with your RCA exercise. As long as you keep going until you hit an effective conclusion the original symptom does not matter.

Some of the examples I will share with you later on will hopefully encourage you to widen your range of applications of RCA.

The answer is not always out 'there'

This final point is the essence of why I wanted to write this book. I believe that the power of root cause problem solving can be realised at any level of an organisation and, for that reason, personal responsibility and control always come to the fore.

There is a great tendency in RCA to find someone to blame and then stop there. You've found the culprit so the job's done. There may be culpability, but there is often a deeper story and part of that story is the responsibility you personally could have taken and / or the actions you did / didn't undertake.

I'm going to expand on this point in a few pages time and share with you some ideas on how you can increase personal responsibility, accountability and ultimately performance via RCA. I did say at the start of this book that this approach isn't for everyone, but it is for you if you are willing to embrace the following phrase:

"Do you want to be right, or do you want results?"
Dennis Stevenson

This phrase makes the point that you can either work on principle (and be right) or be effective and do what it takes get what you need (results). Over time you can shift how your business works so that you can get the results in a better way. If today results aren't forthcoming then embracing personal responsibility further is a route worth considering.

I'll come back to all of these points in due course, but next I am going to give you a recap (or a crash course, depending on your past experience with RCA) on root cause analysis tools.

A recap on root cause problem solving approaches

Although this book is aimed at extending the idea behind root cause analysis, it would be remiss of me not to provide an overview of two of the most popular approaches. I have personally found fishbone analysis and the 5 why method to be incredibly useful, I will share more on my experiences later on.

I have also included two other techniques that I feel complement root cause analysis perfectly, to extend your toolkit.

Fishbone analysis

The fishbone analysis approach is a great way for you to explore cause and effect relationships in your business. It is also wonderfully simple to understand which means that the learning required to successfully use this tool is minimal. Mastery, like most things in life, can take a little longer!

Let me give you an overview of the process.

The starting point is to establish what effect you are trying to resolve. In the diagram below you can see the basic format for a fishbone analysis (and probably understand where it gets its name from!) and that the effect is located on the right hand side.

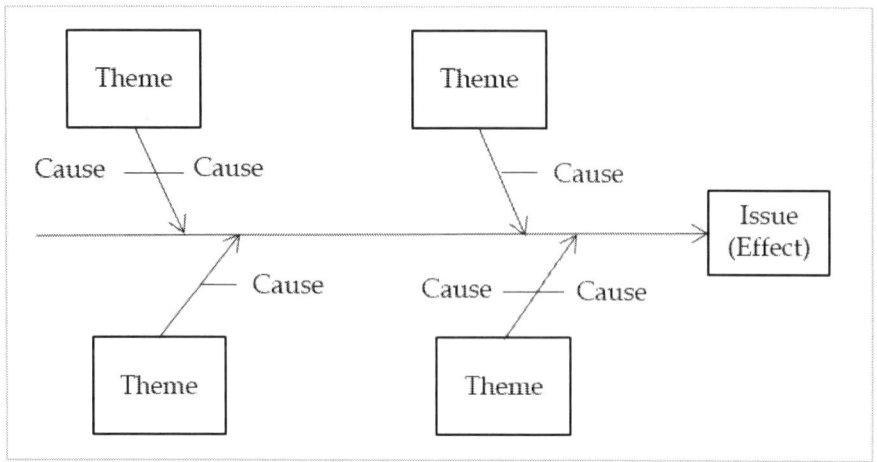

The basic layout for a fishbone diagram, linking cause with effect

The arrows on the diagram are there for you to list out the main causal themes and then the detail of the causes against each theme. As you can see from the example on the next page, it can generate quite a lot of routes to resolve / explore and is a great way to engage the team with RCA.

The themes can be specific to your business, the situation, or you can use a standard heading list to get you started. The four Ms is commonplace, with the Ms standing for Man, Machine, Method and Money. If you are unsure of the themes you want to explore for specific analyses, the four Ms is a good place to start.

Thinking about each theme will allow you to generate the causal factors that could produce the problem you are facing. Listing these out on the diagram allows you to build a picture of what is causing the problem you have in your business. The image below is a summary of an exercise I carried out with one of my client's teams.

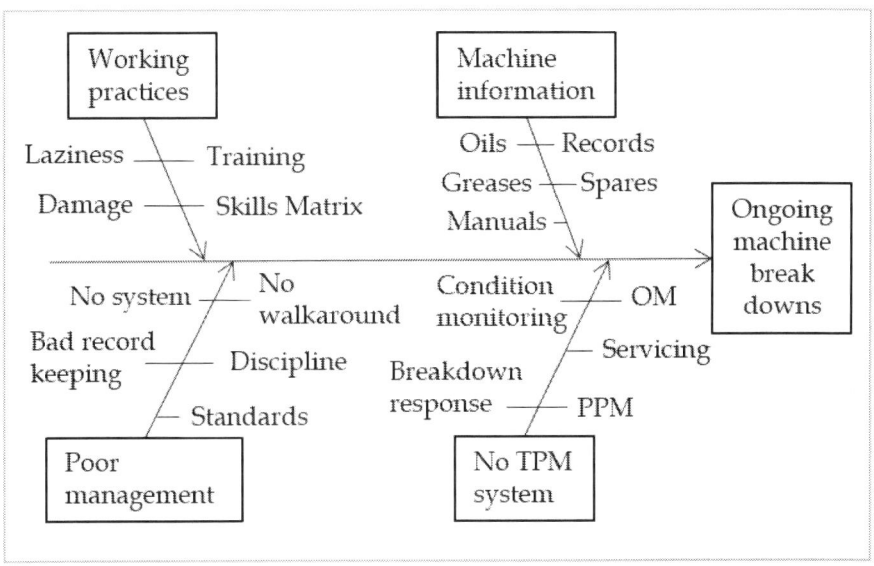

An example of factors affecting machine breakdowns

Usually this approach can generate a large number of improvement tasks and that is one of its benefits. One of the drawbacks is that the items that get listed may not be root causes and could require further investigation. I personally like to use the tool because it is good for getting the team together and getting some quick wins identified.

The next method I am going to provide an overview to, the 5 why method, can help to really dig deep into a specific symptom of a problem. But before I do that, let me tell you about what I think is often a missed opportunity when using fishbone analysis.

Fishbone analysis is often only used on the 'negative past'; something has gone wrong and we need to fix it. An additional way to use this tool is to consider the 'positive future'. Instead of just looking at things you don't want to experience, try analysing something you do want to experience. The image below is reproduced from part of an exercise I was carrying out with a client of mine. Dealing with root cause analysis from this perspective (looking towards future goals rather than at past problems) will help you to change your view and present you with a wide range of improvement opportunities. If you aren't familiar with the term OTIF, it stands for 'On Time In Full' and is a common delivery metric.

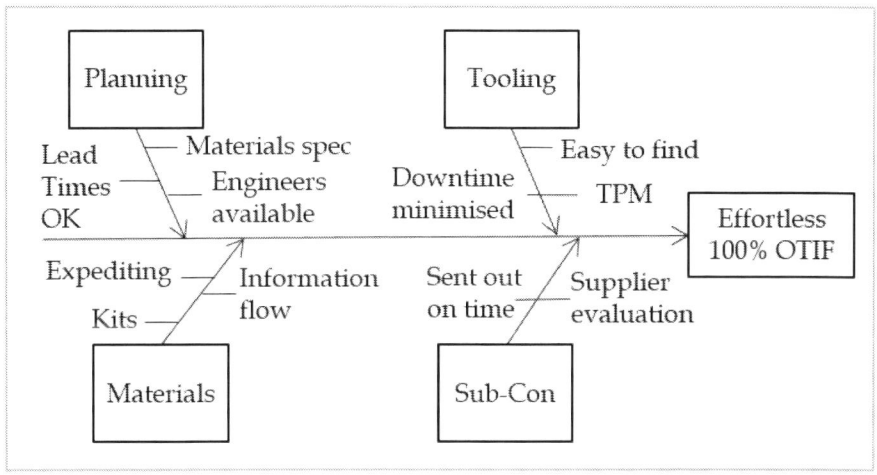

A fishbone used in reverse, focusing on a good effect

I constantly make the point with my clients that it is a different journey to move your business from broken to OK than it is to move it from OK to amazing. Running the fishbone analysis in both directions will help you to overcome this issue by considering both situations.

5 why method

Another really popular method is the '5 why' method. This approach does not need a diagram to accompany it, is great to carry out 'on the fly', and can produce some astounding results. However, I have also seen this tool used poorly and earn a bad name through using blunt questions.

The method is simple enough. Start with a problem your business is facing and ask a 'why?' question about the subject to learn about more about the problem. This procedure is then repeated until you reach a root cause and your analysis is then completed. From here you then put a countermeasure in place to address the root cause so that you can permanently fix the issue you were looking at originally.

The two (poor) applications I regularly see on my travels are:
1. Not drilling down deep enough to find a true root cause. If you end the process prematurely and don't get to the root cause, then you are likely to be left tinkering with symptoms of the real issue. The fix you put in place will not be 100% effective and some other manifestation of the issue will appear at some point in the future.
2. Literally asking 'why?' without any other guidance. If you are facilitating the root cause analysis exercise, then you need to help people find their way through their particular maze. By asking clarifying questions your team will be better at finding a way to dig to the

next level of the analysis. From here you will be able to ask better questions and get to the real root cause.

Let me take these two points and share with you my view on making 5 why an incredible tool for your business by asking a couple of questions.

How do you know when you've reached a root cause?

When you carry out a RCA and you progress through the various layers of the issue, you will notice that the problem shifts from specific symptom-like topics to more generic and broader topics. As you descend through the levels, back to the root, you will most likely hit an 'aha' moment. A flash of the blindingly obvious usually accompanies an effective root cause. My general recommendation here is to not stop digging at an issue until you have had this 'flash' that is often accompanied by you holding your head in your hands!

Five whys is a guidance note. Depending on your questions you might be able to get to the root in fewer hops, or you might need more. If your questions are taking you down a cul-de-sac then it might take a few more "why?" questions to get back on course (after you briefly reverse). If you find yourself with multiple routes to take then make a note of the options, explore one and then the other. It is likely that both routes will lead to the same conclusion if you dig far enough, but best to be certain.

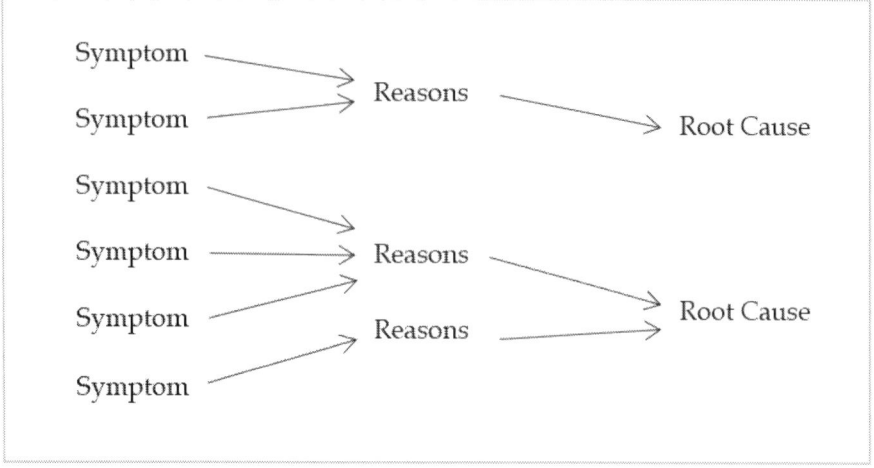

Most symptoms will boil down to only a handful of root causes

The next chapter will extend this idea of digging down further, but for now I suggest that you practice asking good why questions until you hit an 'aha' moment. That leads me nicely on to the other question:

How can you ensure that you ask good why questions?

As I mentioned before I regularly see people ask ineffective why? questions.

There is an engineering acronym called 5W1H, which is a series of question starters:

>Who?
>What?
>Where?
>When?
>Why?
>How?

Let's park the why? question temporarily. If you ask questions with the other starters you will better understand the situation. From here you can ask a really good why? question. The question "why?" on its own can stump a lot of people. A question like 'why does this only happen when the order has more than three items?' can be targeted by the brain more effectively.

I tell my clients to go around the issue with these headings asking the related questions first. When they are ready, they can then ask an effective why question. This approach helps them jump to the next level down in the investigation. At each level the team repeats the who, what, when, where, how questions to produce the next why question. They keep going until they hit their 'aha' moment.

It really is a simple technique that can yield superb results if practiced. The next chapter has a twist on this approach that can make a massive difference both personally and commercially.

Nominal Group Technique (NGT)

This next method is not specifically an RCA technique, but a great method when you have a team of people trying to determine what themes need to form your fishbone diagram.

The basic idea is that you brainstorm all of the issues around a problem, collate them into logical groups and then give the group a name. Voila, you have a set of themes to continue your RCA exercise.

In a little more detail:
- Issue everyone in the team with a set of sticky notes.
- Tell the team what goal / issue / problem you are looking to resolve.
- Ask them to write one cause / related problem / reason per sticky note.

- Ask them to focus on this task for ten minutes.
- After the time has elapsed ask the whole team to put their sticky notes onto a wall / table in the area you are working in.
- As a team review the sticky notes and group similar issues together.
- (If you have a few stragglers that you are unsure what to do with feel free to have an 'other' category.)
- Name each grouping. Each grouping becomes a theme in your RCA exercise.
- Make a note of which themes have more issues within them. This might have no bearing on which theme you wish to tackle first but consider it and then decide.

Despite this not being an RCA method, it is a great way to get a team talking about solving a problem and should shed some light as to what the key themes are. From here you can choose to use the fishbone approach, or the 5 why method, to drill down to uncover the root cause(s).

CCC / 3C

The next tool that I want to share with you is, again, not an RCA method. It is however a superb framework for housing your RCA endeavours.

CCC (or 3C) stands for 'Concern Cause Countermeasure'.
It is a brilliant method for capturing ideas and then dealing with them in a systematic fashion. You will observe that the middle C is 'cause', and this is where our RCA methods fit into place.

Concern	Cause	Countermeasure

The basic layout of a CCC document

As you can see, the CCC format is very simple. For this reason it is a great way to get your entire team to contribute if they haven't before. At the outset all you need them to do is to bring the grumbles, gripes and concerns to the table. If the solution is obvious then by all means define a countermeasure (the action you are going to take to correct the situation). If it isn't then this is when you put your RCA hat on and figure out what is the underlying cause of this symptom.

Encourage your team to bring issues to the table, work on the root causes as a team and then agree on an action plan.

See, CCC is simple after all.

But, how do we put this all together?

Tying all the approaches together

I'm sure that in your own mind you can see how you can stack these different approaches to give you a range of applications.

Let me run through a few of the combinations that I have found to be useful in the past.

1. CCC and 5 why

Sharing the CCC approach with either my own teams (in a

previous employed life) or with my client teams I have found this combination a really potent one to draw out issues from within the business. Many times I will see managers recoil when they hear yet another issue raised by their team. You've probably heard the phrase 'don't bring me problems, bring me solutions!' being used. Whilst it is preferable that people hand you a workable solution on a plate (and then hopefully implement it once you approve it), this rarely happens.

Using the CCC approach you can systematically work through the concerns as described earlier. Any simple fixes can be identified, prioritised and implemented. Anything that requires a little bit more digging (usually because the solution isn't obvious, or the solutions put forward all have their own problems) is a prime candidate for 5 why.

When you carry out a 5 why RCA exercise using the concerns listed you will likely find that the solution to your root cause will address many other concerns you have on your list. Mark them off and keep going until you have cleared your list of concerns and are left with the makings of an action plan.

2. NGT and 5 why

When the team seem to have too many problems to deal with

at once, putting them into logical groups using NGT (the Nominal Group Technique) and then addressing one of the symptoms using 5 why is both an effective and efficient way to proceed.

Once you have identified a root cause, review the rest of the issues / symptoms you have under the same heading and see if the solution will address these symptoms. Tick off the dealt with items and repeat the process with anything you feel hasn't been addressed. Repeat this activity for the rest of the logical groupings.

3. Fishbone and 5 why

When you have a problem to solve and want to use a standardised approach this combination works a treat. If you agree on some standard themes for your fishbone (such as the four Ms mentioned earlier) you can deploy this approach as part of your standard business improvement toolkit.

Brainstorming the causal factors against each theme (e.g. Man, Machine, Method and Money) is a great way for the team to start drawing out avenues of interest. Once you have completed this brain dump then you can use the 5 why approach to really delve into one or two of the sub-symptoms that you think have merit. As I mentioned earlier, if you dig to a true root cause then your solution will eradicate many of the other symptoms you have listed.

This chapter of the book was intended as a brief overview of root cause analysis. Hopefully it has either given you an introduction to a handful of methods or given you a useful refresher. The important point I want to reiterate is that whatever technique you use to understand the true root cause behind an issue, you must keep going until you reach that 'aha' moment. When the whole topic becomes clear and you are confident that your solution will properly remedy the situation then you will have my blessing to proceed! All too often, there are ideal solutions just sitting one hop away from us. If we get past the current level of thinking to that final level, it can make a massive difference to the effectiveness of your solution.

Later in this book I will share with you some anonymised case studies that will expand this point. But, for now, let us move on to the reason I decided to write this book.

The idea

This chapter is the essence of why I wanted to write this book. As I said at the outset, many times I witness RCA being carried out to point the finger and blame. A simple flip of this idea can make RCA an even more powerful tool for you and your business. And, as I said in the introduction, this idea isn't for everyone. If you embrace it, however, I am confident that you will find great ways to apply this 'RCA bolt on' successfully and see some really impressive results.

Personal responsibility

The extension I am referring to is all around personal responsibility. Whatever the solution we arrive at when carrying out an RCA exercise, there is always something that can be done at a personal level. It is very easy to point the finger elsewhere and say that is where the root cause lies, but much harder to reflect on ourselves to consider what part we played in the whole affair.

At each level within an organisation there is always a degree of control. The magnitude of this control might be a lot less at lower levels (usually execution) compared to the senior levels (usually policy), but there is control nonetheless. The ability to identify and define these levels of control will depend on who you engage with during your investigation and, of course, their willingness to be open about the process. As I said at the outset, this RCA extension is not everyone's cup of tea.

If you accept that actions originate from thought, then that firmly puts personal responsibility in the centre of the discussion when considering a true root cause. If we can encourage more people to realise their personal responsibility then control at all levels, as well as performance, increases.

We / They

I sat in a meeting earlier this year with a senior leadership team. The owner of the company and I had just visited one of their clients and we got some rather negative feedback. The owner was furious as all the controls and procedures that should have been implemented appeared to have been bypassed during one single client experience. This meeting with the leadership team was to ask 'what can we do to improve?'.

The team played with the issues and then talked about the

actions that 'we' could undertake. Not a single person said 'I' and this is a shift that I think many businesses could benefit from.

After a few minutes of these 'we' statements I asked if there should be anyone else around the table. The team responded 'no' and asked me why I would ask that. When I explained that not a single person had taken responsibility for the actions, they seemed initially surprised and then started to propose what they, as individuals, would do. Generalised comments sound OK, but they often don't generate results. There was a perfect opportunity in the meeting for people to realise the things that they were responsible for that they had failed to execute and declare them as actions. This approach, even at a senior level, can be hard.

If you're reading this and shaking your head, thinking that this is what people should be doing, then I agree with you. But there are too many experiences I have been part of (or witnessed) where this just isn't the case. Talking to colleagues and other businesses the same topic comes up time and time again; generally we point the finger at 'them' and talk about 'us'. If we talk about ourselves and ensure that control is seized at an individual level, wherever this might be, performance will improve.

I

When we talk about 'I' we get to put our personal 'house in order'. There is no longer a total reliance on other people having to do something in order to achieve a result, we are able to exert our own influence in all kinds of matters.

The phrase I referred to earlier, that has stuck with me is 'do you want to be right, or do you want results?'. This is the same issue, it is very easy for me to agree with anyone why something shouldn't have to happen, but if the results are important then we need to take the appropriate actions. I agree with my clients that they shouldn't have to chase their colleagues to close out non-conformance reports. I agree with my clients that they shouldn't have to build reporting structures for their members of staff. I agree that they shouldn't have to ask them about their process management. But if results are at the foremost then let's put to one side what is 'right' and focus on what is 'effective'.

If we focus on what is effective then we can move to efficient later on. We can back off all of the above points once the right habits and routines have been established within the business. The chasing of non-conformance reports can lessen, process management can start to take care of itself and reports will be right, once the groove has been made.

If you are experiencing problems, then doing the right things overrules being right. As you have probably guessed, if you extend this idea to your team then they might start to take some personal responsibility. Of course, some people won't see the issue with what they are doing and therefore won't want to engage. I am writing this text for you, the someone that is interested in this approach. Through your actions results can cascade.

We work with imperfect systems. The whole benefit of having people in our business can seem to be outweighed by the negatives at times. Embracing this idea at your level (wherever that is) in your business and emanating the results outwards is a good strategy and if you can get more people to take part with taking responsibility the faster you can see significant change.

Dig to the core, stop at you

To apply this idea to your business you just need one minor change to your RCA approach. When you think you have reached a root cause (accompanied by that 'aha' moment) keep going a little further until you can declare your involvement with the situation. When you have reached 'you' then you have something powerful to work with. Decisions that have or haven't been taken, or thinking that you have or haven't done, has the potential for quick and powerful changes if you can recognise them.

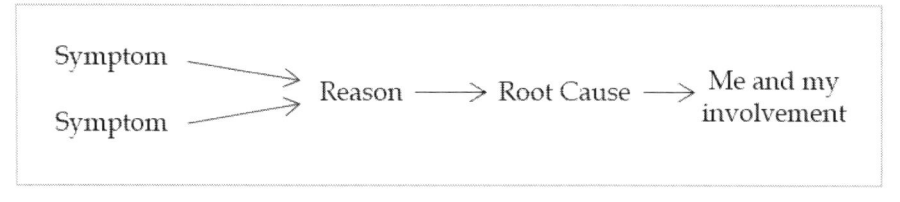

Symptom
Symptom ⟶ Reason ⟶ Root Cause ⟶ Me and my involvement

The logical extension of RCA – where are you in the issue?

When you get to the 'I' part of the RCA then you will have gotten to something really basic and effective. If the nucleus of every action is from a thought then that can only take place in the heads of the people involved with the situation. We need to get to 'I' in order to maximise effectiveness.

The impact of 'I' will be different at each level of the

organisation. At the lower levels the realisation might be that notification to higher levels, or escalation of issues, could have been done but wasn't. At the middle levels there might be realisations about how situations are managed. At the senior levels there are likely to be conversations about what kinds of things are missing in the business and what decision are and aren't being made.

Two-prong your thinking when you reach your root cause and you will have a powerful approach to improving the performance of your business. One part of this will be focused on the hard process type changes your business needs to make. The other will be a personal / style change of some sort.

Max out control

By thinking this little bit further about personal responsibility, how you are directly involved with the situation, you increase the level of control taking place in the business. There are many times that things may seem out of our control, but there is always a degree of control.

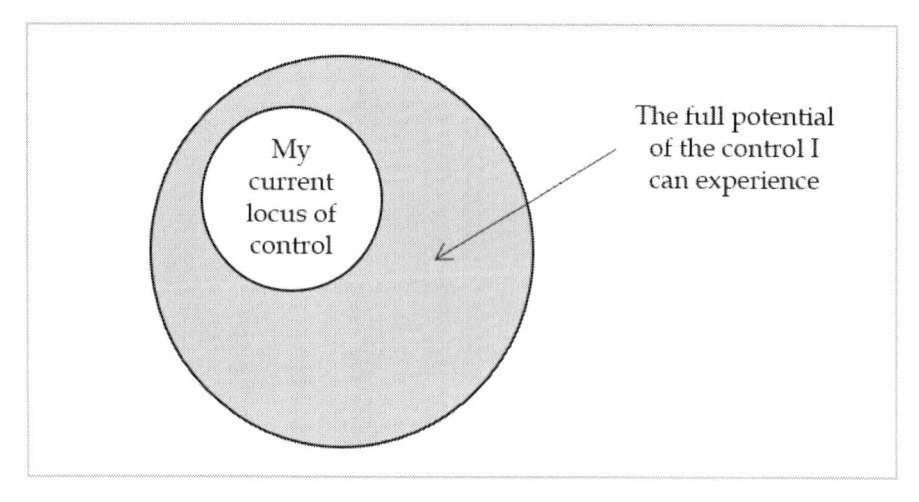

We rarely exercise our full control

Exercising our full control is a key consideration to improving our personal and (hence) business performance. By extending the RCA finish point to 'I', we move towards fully utilising our control which increases our chances of high performance in our organisation.

My objective, when working with clients, is that we max out the control being exerted at each level of the organisation. Here, everyone is taking control and responsibility and pulling in one direction. As I said before, our businesses are imperfect systems and correcting this is a general objective. If enough people engage with the idea in this book and take their piece of the control jigsaw, then our system imperfections can be managed.

Sure, the person who can ultimately change your processes might be in another department. Your control to influence that process' results sits with you right now. That is why we must get to 'I' when we carry out our root cause analyses.

The questions

At this point I hope that you can see the power of extending root cause analysis into the realm of personal responsibility.

The questions to ask at the end of an RCA exercise are simple but powerful. This chapter covers this type of question and will hopefully give you the twist that can make a big difference to your personal effectiveness, as well as that of your team and your business.

At root cause

When you have reached the root cause from your investigation (i.e. when you have reached that 'aha' moment), there are two good questions to contemplate:

What did you do that helped lead to this situation?

What didn't you do that helped lead to this situation?

I recommend that you answer both questions so that you cover both perspectives. The next chapter includes some anonymised case studies that will give examples of these questions in use.

As you can see, they are really basic questions. They focus the mind back to the idea of taking personal responsibility and, when answered honestly, can produce actions that can make a fundamental shift in terms of how you operate and how the business will perform going forward.

Can you imagine what would happen if even just a few members of your team embraced this idea? I have been lucky enough to work with a number of people over the years that have 'got' this idea and, when they put 'I' back in the centre of what they were doing, found that their performance, and the performance of their team, soared.

As I write this, I am reflecting on the number of complaints my clients make about their teams 'always finding a reason for something not to work'. Helping your teams shift their assessment of the situation from 'them' to 'I' is hard, but it is an option to get out of this loop. It takes time and I have personally experienced my teams and my client's teams changing their approach. Don't expect this to happen overnight but, if you do persist, the results can be worth it.

These questions are tough. They require you to address your own personal shortcomings. We all have them, so let's get on with admitting them and moving forward. You don't have to declare them publicly either; I would never ask that of you. I also believe that actions speak louder than words, so let's keep to that and use the reflection for good rather than personal embarrassment.

During solution creation

The other questions that you need to ask lead on from the reflection of what you did, or didn't, do.

The questions are:

What could I do?

What will I do?

The first question is all about idea generation. List out the options you have available to you.

The second question is decision making. With all of the options you have available to you, what are you going to do about it?

As with all options, some will be more effective than others, some will be more efficient, and some will be easier. Choose the option that gives you the best combination (the best results with the least effort and hassle!).

The last question seals off the RCA exercise fully, putting personal responsibility into effect.

Moving from decision into action

Following through with your commitment requires action. There are many ways that you can do this and here are a few of my favourite ideas, so that you can get better results faster:

Create an action plan

Make sure that you have an action plan. This can be as basic as you feel comfortable with but should include a few essential items:

- The action itself should be clear to anyone reading the document and should stand on its own.
- Only one person should be responsible for the action. Other people may deliver part of the action, but one person needs to be in charge of getting the job done.
- A deadline is essential. Without some kind of focus on time, it is likely that tasks will drift and improvements won't be made.
- Other items that you might consider include the status of the tasks, the deliverables and a notes / update area.

A simple spreadsheet can work well for this, as can many of the online planner tools that are available.

Engage your team

Doing the work all on your own is going to take longer, require more effort and produce a limited outcome. When you engage your team, you make the process of change a less lonely task. I have had the benefit of working with many talented and fun people over the years and they can make the whole process of change a more productive experience.

Give your team a handful of good reasons to get involved with the change that you need to put in place and give them the opportunity to get involved. At first you might find it quite hard to get people involved in 'extra work', but this can be countered by having good reasons to make the improvement.

Ensure that you have a good cross section of people, skills and experiences on your team and let them get involved with the planning and execution of the actions.

Keep the action(s) visible

We live in an age where many things are digital. Digital often means that data and information is stored on computers and mobile devices. A key to consider when making improvements is to keep your number one improvement highly visible. The more often you see it the higher the chance that you'll do something about it. This might mean putting up an action plan in a really obvious place in your office or adding the actions to a regular meeting so that you keep on talking about them.

Use whatever strategy makes sense to you, just make sure that you don't hide the actions away from your team.

Use visual management to mark progress

Following on from making your actions visible is the importance of considering some kind of progress measurement. Keeping your team informed as to where you are with reaching the objective will help with making progress. Simple methods such as colouring in boxes that denote progress or using a red / amber / green (RAG) against the project actions to indicate progress are good basic ways to help your team take part more easily.

The approach you take doesn't need to be complicated in order to be effective. The team should know how well they are doing, in terms of making progress, without the need for lengthy analysis.

Set up a routine to review progress

Making progress with improvement activity is more effective when there is a routine to back it up. Looking only occasionally at the improvement actions and periodically pushing improvements doesn't reliably produce results. If you want to improve the business, then a drip feed of little and often is a better approach. This drip feed, over time, can become a raging torrent. It might start small but through a consistent approach this can change as momentum gathers.

I find that most routines work best when the frequency is high at the start and then relaxed to find the right tempo for the business. It is usually easier to relax the frequency once you have started something new rather than the other way around. Also, there is a good chance that you will have some immediate issues to address, so a push in this area will most likely benefit everyone at the outset.

Developing effective routines (or habits) is something many businesses have difficulty with. That said, I also find that most businesses have some existing activities that happen like clockwork such as regular management meetings. Appending a very brief review of improvement actions to a regular management meeting can be all it takes to make continuous improvement a routine activity.

Your business may require that you hold a separate meeting, due to time constraints in the other meetings. Your ability to improve your business will be proportional to your ability to keep the regular meeting slot happening. Change requires discipline (in most cases) and the message that your business gets from having a routine improvement meeting will naturally cascade.

If you form a routine around the review of improvement actions, you will see other benefits for your business appear via the improved discipline.

Define what you will experience at the end

Another good approach is to gain some clarity around what you want to experience at the end of the improvement activity. Defining this, and then sharing with your team, is a great communication method and improves your chances of getting what you want / need at the end.

When improvement goals are set there is often a vagueness around the results that are required. This isn't surprising when you consider that many employees are just desperate to get away from a poor situation; anything can seem better.

Taking a little more time to articulate the outcome is well worth it and doesn't have to be difficult. If you want 'it' to come in a green box at the end, tell everyone about the green box! If you are unsure about spelling out what you want, try using the 5W1H approach we discussed earlier on:

Who / What / Where / When / Why / How

In this case the 'why' element is a useful reminder for the team regarding the importance / purpose of the change. You can re-use the prompts as many times as you require to cover all your points. If you aren't bothered about how something will arrive or be produced, then leave it open. Just make sure that you get the essentials defined.

The above comment about a green box came from a meeting I had with the owner of a business who had set his team an objective. They carried out the objective's tasks over a period of several months and then presented the outcome. It wasn't what the owner wanted, but it did fulfil the specification when looking at it objectively. There were a number of expectations that hadn't been spelled out and this left a frustrated team and a frustrated owner. In this case the 'what' and 'how' could have come into play to guide the team to a few of the items that would have met expectations.

Let me expand briefly on the 5W1H elements:

Who do I want to present the information / do I want involved with the activity?

What do I want to see at the end / want included (or excluded) in the activity (or scope) of the improvement activity?

Where do I want you to look at and explore?

When do I want the results by / do I expect milestones to be reached?

Why are we doing this improvement (business case)?

How do I want you to approach this improvement?

Hopefully you can see how these prompts stack up to help articulate an effective improvement outline which will ensure that the outcome is the one that is wanted.

Adjust your course as required

Being stuck rigidly on one course of action is a double-edged sword. In many cases you will need to persevere and carry on doggedly to get the results you are seeking. At other times changing to an alternative path is the right strategy.

Being able to think ahead several steps is useful here; don't just change to a different path because it is easier. If you end up in a cul-de-sac then you will have to expend more energy and effort to get back to where you branched off.

Let me give you a quick example. I was working with two sister businesses that were revamping the way they scheduled their factories. We had a plan for an identical method to be implemented at both sites and it wasn't working at one of the sites. There was nothing wrong with the approach, but it didn't seem to be gelling for them. They wanted to do something else and, in the end, it is the results that matter.

I agreed with the senior leadership team on a change of approach. The first site would carry on with the original plan. The second site would tweak their approach, but it would have to include certain requirements and they had to gain sign off for the new approach before implementation.

At the end of the implementation we had two documented,

fully functional and effective systems. They were close enough in operation to still allow transfer of staff as and when required. I would have preferred to have had a standardised approach to the activity, but delivering robust results were more important. Knowing when to stick and when to adjust is an important tool in anyone's toolbox.

Celebrate and move on

The last point I want to make in this chapter is about celebrating. Remembering to stop and celebrate the results you have achieved can really help to bring the team with you and improve the rate of future results.

A lot of hard work and effort goes into making improvements happen within a business and recognition is vital. I'm not necessarily talking about pay rises and pats on the back. Realising that you have achieved something and not letting the moment for praise pass everyone by is vital for the long term.

Creating a timeline of achievement, or some other way of looking back and recalling how far you have come can be really motivational for all involved. When you are working day to day in the business it can be really easy to miss how much better things are becoming. Another way to do this is tag this reflection into a periodic management meeting (quarterly or half-yearly is a good frequency).

I hope that these eight points will help you to be more effective at implementing change. When you have identified what you need to change, and what you personally need to adjust, then getting the results is what it's all about.

In the next chapter I am going to share with you some examples from my clients that have had their epiphanies whilst exploring this twist on RCA.

Stories

At this point I hope that you can see how adding a small twist to your RCA activities can potentially make a big difference to the results you can realise.

So far this has been a nice idea, hasn't it? To try and emphasise how much improvement this change can make, let me share with you a handful of stories from my own experience when working and doing consultancy.

Painful customer feedback

One of my clients has a well-developed client feedback process. At the end of every project the owner visits the client and follows the prescribed client feedback agenda. From this the business finds out what went well and what didn't go so well. It's part of their continuous improvement process and usually yields some learning points (as well as repeat business).

During a particular period one year there were quite a number of projects coming to a close and we carried out eight of these reviews in a row. From these sessions there was a variety of improvement points to consider. However, some of these items needed a little more input than just the client review meeting and we decided to pull the senior leadership team together. With the team we carried out a root cause analysis exercise on a handful of the priority items that had been raised by the clients.

When I opened the director's RCA session, they all sat back waiting for me to do something. Instead I assured them that they would be doing the heavy lifting and proceeded to explain the 5 why method (linked with the 5W1H approach). I also made a point that they had to keep going with their digging until they were pointing a finger straight back at themselves.

It was slow going at first. There was lots of finger pointing (at other people) and lots of complaining, but they persisted. They kept on going until they reached some fairly fundamental points. They realised that they had failed to introduce specific activities within their business. They realised that some of their decisions had yielded unexpected results. They also realised that some of the methods they had used with their direct reports hadn't been as effective as they had hoped.

After their epiphanies they came up with a simple action plan. They had driven their root cause thinking towards themselves so they were in control of the actions. They had got to root cause, so the actions were relatively straightforward. The efforts they had made to dig down to themselves during the process was more than justified by the effectiveness, simplicity and swiftness of the improvement plan.

Over a period of months their results changed. Their eagerness to fill positions and start projects adjusted and the feeling of being rushed in the business started to dissipate. What seemed like delays within the business' activities were controlled pauses and did not negatively affect their project performance. Decisions that hadn't been made, or made late before, were now occurring at the right times and this started to save time at the back end of the projects. The improvements were noticed by the staff within the business and this helped the senior management team to implement further changes. During this time, we slowly worked our way through the actions we identified during the RCA session and a number of benefits started to appear:

- On time delivery of the projects moved in the right direction. There was notably less panic towards the end of the project's life.

- Customer satisfaction improved. The grumbles and complaints decreased because of the changes the directors made to their own approach. This naturally led to a higher level of repeat business being won.
- The teams below the directors started to behave differently and became more effective. Largely this was down to two things; the senior team leading by example and the expectations of the team's compliance with the process made crystal clear.

It was an interesting experience to watch unfold. Small things that had been in the control of the directors had become clear to them during the RCA process. This in turn led to a very straightforward action plan. Project performance was measured as a secondary activity. Executing the actions and routines was the primary measure. This was very much a case of 'we'll do the right things and see what the results are'. The monitoring of the results became a separate discussion and the working environment became much healthier. The rest of the business' teams then followed their lead and noticed a (slightly) less hectic work life.

It really can be astounding what results a business can produce when the RCA drills down to the 'I' level willingly!

A decision to stop running around like a headless chicken!

Many years ago I ran a factory operation that was somewhat of a poisoned chalice when I took on the role. I knew that our output was erratic at times and that our on time delivery performance wasn't as good as it needed to be, but when I was offered the role I took it as I was planning to leave the company and this role would look good on my CV.

After making this move from engineering across to production, I soon became proficient in over promising our production capacity to our customers. The order book was in a state of chaos and I receive the brunt of the customer phone calls / complaints. "When will you be shipping my order?" "The last week of the month!" was the usual ping pong conversation… I conservatively estimate that I would commit around 3000% of our capacity in that final week of the month!

There were so many problems to deal with. There were also so many people that weren't doing their job properly. It was unbelievable and I found myself slipping into the same old patterns that the other managers were in – blaming everyone except myself.

This pattern went on for several months. And, as you would expect, it didn't get me any decent results. The lead time was still way out at twenty weeks. The OTIF (On Time In Full) delivery performance was still bumbling around the 20% mark. The customers were still unhappy and so was I. The only strange thing was that everyone else in the business seemed okay about it as it was normal and therefore within their 'comfort zone'.

My unhappiness peaked and one Friday afternoon I decided that I didn't want this episode of serious underperformance on my CV; I decided to do something different. I performed a similar analysis to the one I have explained in this book. I looked at my key problems and dug at them until I reached the control that I had in my possession. For every issue that I reached I took a sheet of paper and made a heading that captured the control that I hadn't exercised or had performed badly.

Within an hour or two I had sixteen headings on my wall. These were sixteen mini projects that were all in my control to implement and manage that would have some impact on the poor delivery performance and customer satisfaction. Not every problem in the business would be fixed, I realised this, but I would be able to exert my maximal level of influence in the business.

As I stood staring at my handywork I realised that there was a clear priority in the plans. I marked this up and then made a commitment to myself, to start my working day working on my plans in the sequence I had agreed with myself. When I completed an action plan, I checked the sequence again to ensure that it made sense and then I carried on. Some days I got a lot of work done and some days I got very little done, but I accomplished something towards my plans. I still had the day job to contend with but starting the day with my plans made a real difference. Starting the day was under my control, how I finished it didn't always seem to be!

Within six months the manufacturing operation had moved from around 20% OTIF up to a rolling average of 98%. The production lead time dropped from nearly twenty weeks to just over three. The team seemed happier and our natural capacity rose (the business was eventually able to output nearly three times the volume of orders with no extra staff or overtime). There were battles on the way, it certainly wasn't a smooth ride, but my decision and understanding of control had a notable impact. If you want to know more about this particular journey see the further reading section later in this book.

Can all of the business activities really link?

One of my clients talked to me one day about some of their frustrations. They grumbled to me that the management team on the other half of the business were constantly making decisions that negatively affected them. The manager I was speaking to was responsible for production. The half of the business he was complaining about was the commercial / sales arm of the business. I could understand his frustration; the sales force kept on selling the type of work that his team weren't great at doing. We discussed what the sales team's purpose was and selling production capacity was most likely to be their number one priority. It was easy to complain about the situation, but that isn't the way to get results (and certainly isn't the focus of this book!). The frustrated manager agreed to look more deeply into this issue.

We gathered a small team together and carried out the RCA exercise. There was a lot of debate within the team about where to start so we began with the Nominal Group Technique (NGT) to gain consensus on where we were starting. The exercise threw up a number of key issues for the team and this was captured as a fishbone diagram, the themes now defined. The team took one issue from the biggest area of concern and undertook a 5 why analysis. This is where the fun began.

The usual experience unfolded. They asked a number of good questions to contextualise the issues and then asked a meaningful "why?" question. This led them to pointing the finger of failure at another party. I had explained to them the need to keep on digging until the answer was a more basic and fundamental issue. They did so until they eventually ended up with something that they could deal with, that was in their control.

The major frustration that they were trying to better understand was the mismatch between the available skills on a shift and the work content that was being won by the sales team. Their conclusion, eventually, was that the way that they managed their skills matrix and training was inadequate; their team couldn't cope with the range of work being pushed their way. This in its own right is a notable root cause issue to resolve, but as the team had grasped the idea of taking full control we persisted and dug further.

After brainstorming all of the activities around this issue that they could control, one of the team offered this little gem. The production team could speak with the commercial team and keep them abreast of what skills were available at any point in time. They were talking about generic availability as a team, not just individuals. From some further investigation by the team, to understand how the sales team operated, they found out that the sales team would have many different kinds of opportunities they could pursue at any point in time. Whilst this might not seem like a revelation to anyone reading this from a sales function, the production team hadn't joined the dots together. By asking what was in their control and how it could improve the original issue they had their 'flash of the blindingly obvious'.

The production team devised a simple way to inform the sales and commercial team what their skills and capacity availability was on a regular basis. Although this did not stop the sales team trying to win every sale that was possible (and why should they stop? In this case it was a great problem to have!), they did correlate the sales activity more closely with the skills and resources the business had available. Whilst I could go on further at talk about the contract review process and higher-level sales and operations planning activities, the point of this example is that the production team gained a new awareness of the control and input they could have to a seemingly unsolvable issue.

During the process of the RCA exercise the team developed a more effective way to update their skills matrix, found some better ways to use the skills matrix as an ongoing management tool and linked in with their sister department more effectively.

We are a team (no, honestly!)

I was once asked to join a board meeting at one of my clients' to give my perspective on how the Board worked together. This was quite an awkward conversation because of the lack of teamwork I had seen up to that point. The conversation itself had no real bearing on the work I had recently completed for them but, as I had got to understand them more through the life of the project, I accepted the invite to the board meeting.

The meeting started off pretty well; we recapped on the highs and lows of my project and where the business had now got to. Then the question about how they worked together as a team reared its head. I chose my words carefully (I was hoping to work with them again in the future!) and said that in public they seemed to work well but appeared dysfunctional when they weren't together in public. I shared the limited view I had of them and they went quiet. I had seen them passing notes to each other, grumbling about each other when the others weren't there, saying they didn't agree with each other's plans and wouldn't support each other… you get the picture.

My polite spin on these comments were deliberated and then the Chairman spoke…

"Bollocks!"

I paused a moment, deciding how best to respond and said,

"How bollocks?"

There was a temporary look of disbelief on the Chairman's face and then thankfully one of the other directors chipped in.

"Well, you do pass me notes under my door…"

There were a few stilted moments whilst the directors threw their metaphorical rocks at each other and then they turned their attention to every other person in the business that had failed in some way. This carried on for a few minutes and then I asked them about the results they were producing and influencing themselves. You could imagine that this was a tricky situation, but I persevered.

One of the directors liked the phrase often attributed to Ghandi, "we must be the change we wish to see in the world" and thankfully that gave me something to hang onto in this conversation. I used this phrase and somehow got the three of them to mull this over. I stressed the significance of their actions, even on the small things, and we started to review some of the comments that they had just made.

Over the next half an hour they seemed to make some progress with their discussion. By the end of the meeting they had agreed on some actions that they were going to take for them to be more effective as a team and a range of actions that would help their teams to perform more effectively. This ranged from ensuring decisions were made more swiftly through to participating in activities to which they had previously only given lip service.

They were right, there were problems within the business that weren't directly caused by them. Thankfully, by the end of the meeting, they now had some different ways to look at these problems and how they worked together as a team. Did they transform their own working relationship so that they became a super case study? No. From my viewpoint they did enough to become functional; they put the business first and made some notable operational changes and improvements. I'm pleased that the changes they made did make a significant improvement to their performance.

The changes that they made to the business, based on them seeing themselves at the centre of the problems, led them to support their business to rise from the worst performer in their supply chain league table to the best. It took them about six months and the transformation was remarkable. Not only did they become the number one performer, but this change in performance led them to win additional work that they previously didn't have access to.

Opportunities

As you have read this book, I hope that you have started to spot some of the opportunities that are present in your business. Being flexible with the idea of drilling down your root cause analysis until you find yourself can conjure many areas where minor tweaks could lead to major gains. This chapter includes a handful of areas that I have found my clients (and myself) have gained the most by looking at.

Personal development

One of the most obvious gains to be had is that around personal development. None of us are perfect and everyone is prone to making the occasional mistake. If you drill down past the symptoms of a business problem and eventually find the part of the story that you played, you may just find a personal development opportunity.

Personal development improvements might include:

Time management

If the root cause you arrive at revolves around time and how you have managed it thus far, then this could well be an opportunity for improvement. There is a good chance that most businesses have experienced poor time management. From a personal effectiveness standpoint if you can better prioritise the decision making and execution portions of your working day then you have the potential to improve your personal effectiveness.

Simple, well thought out routines are often an improvement option when RCA reveals a time related issue. The routines can often prompt activities, working as a trigger, to ensure that key tasks and routines operate in a timely fashion. Whatever your particular time management issues are, reconfiguring how you plan and use your time will no doubt bear fruit in terms of becoming more effective.

Being assertive

One of the simplest outcomes many of my client's staff experience when carrying out this personal slant on RCA is around being assertive. Problems that they have experienced in the past may have boiled down to many things, but their 'input' certainly affected the outcome.

The best example of this is escalating problems. Something is wrong in the business and the matter has been raised by the individual to their line manager (or someone similar). The issue then gets left alone and nothing happens. Does this sound familiar?

Conversations around this are always similar. I empathise with where they are coming from too; everyone is busy, and it is not a usual expectation that you manage other people that aren't directly under your control. Let me expand briefly with an example. A few weeks ago, I was talking with a team of middle managers. One of their teams had a problem with moving material because the overhead crane was out of commission. They had raised the issue with the maintenance technician who had added it to their list of duties. Other duties were being carried out and this specific crane repair was not being organised and completed. Weeks passed before it came up in our conversation. I asked them about what control they had over the situation and we moved from 'none' to 'some'. It was in their control to be able to keep asking for updates, offering to help and escalating the issue ever upwards until the results were achieved. This group argued that they shouldn't have to 'micro-manage' the situation and, in principle, I agree. However, going back to the phrase 'do you want to be right or do you want results?', what did they want?

They wanted their shops to be able to use the crane because the cost of downtime was notable (it was in the region of £300 per hour in terms of non-productive time being generated in the affected areas). So, whilst I agree with the principle of not having to manage others the results need to be taken care of.

This team changed their approach to maximising their control and influence without worrying about being right. They became more effective as a team and their performance tracked upwards alongside their minor change in behaviour. It didn't take much to look at their work environment differently and the way that they asserted themselves (instead of being victims of other people's poor performance) was relatively low effort.

Moving on from this example, asserting yourself will not always produce the results that you want. This point is all about giving yourself the best chance of getting the outcome. It might well be the case that the very issue that you are wanting resolved is not a high enough priority for the business' limited resources. As a minimum you will be able to find out the relative priority for the issue you are trying to resolve. At best, you will start to see issues that don't get resolved quickly being completed at a much quicker pace.

Finding an issue around being assertive from your RCA is a real opportunity for you to capitalise on.

Planning

The quality and frequency of planning is an ongoing theme for many businesses. If your RCA exercise points the finger towards your abilities to plan activities in your business, then I urge you to embrace this opportunity.

The act of stopping and putting some time to one side in order to think things through is enough for many businesses to experience a massive jump in terms of effectiveness. There are many planning systems available to us nowadays, but if you aren't using any particular methodology, then just stopping, thinking and organising is enough for most of us.

There is a saying that every minute spent in planning saves you ten in execution, and whilst I am not sure on the numbers involved I do know what happens if you don't engage with planning! If the topic of planning comes up with my clients, I am usually faced with comments such as "I don't have time for planning" or "I don't know what needs to be planned". These are the same clients that seem to carry out the most rework and travel the longest paths to complete their projects.

I think that the two are linked…

Every business that I have worked with that has developed a simple planning approach that suits their culture and sector have improved their performance. I hope that you take this opportunity too and, if that means delaying the work slightly at the start, it might be very worthwhile. To qualify that statement; delaying the start of an activity in order to get it right often leads to moving faster through the rest of the activities. I recall a group complaining about one of their team taking time at the start of shift to prepare their working area. The individual in question produced more than anyone else in the team by a significant margin. What was being complained about was them not 'mucking in' like everyone else did. What they weren't recognising was that a small amount of preparation led to far greater results. This team member was thinking through what they had in front of them and figuring out the most efficient way to work. After our conversation the rest of the team realised that this was time well spent.

I could give you countless other examples of how a little bit of planning can improve performance, but I have a feeling that you know exactly what I am talking about. Enjoy improving your planning skills!

Communication

It is highly likely that the topic of communication will appear at some point during your RCA exercises. When you drill down far enough, you may find that there are some opportunities to change how you communicate with your team. The main communication issues that I find my clients talking to me about include the clarity of instructions, the frequency of communication and the communication vehicles used. Let me quickly run through these three areas.

With regards to clarity of instructions, the biggest point I see here is sharing the detail in the right areas. I keep telling my clients that 'if you expect your team to discuss their improvement actions every day then you need to tell them'. If there are some key details to share with your team then don't leave them out. This is another application of the 80/20 rule (where 20% of your actions lead to 80% of your results); you don't have to provide the 'nitty gritty' for everything, just the few areas that count. The other point I see around this issue is ensuring that the other people fully understand the instructions. I'm sure that you have also experienced your team saying that they understand the instructions and then walking away and doing something entirely different. The only way I have found around this problem is to get the individual / team to present their methodology for completing a task when it is something new in order to clarify whether they understand or not. However, I would only do this if they had a track record of not following instructions. This usually clears out the misunderstandings and helps confirm that your instructions are clear.

The frequency of communication is often linked to how busy and how organised the rest of the working day is. Regular communications are easier when the stresses and strains of the normal working day aren't in the way. The real test, like many other regular management activities, is what happens to your communication level when you are being stretched. Developing a strategy to deal with this and streamlining your communication approach is a good plan of action. For example:
- If you find yourself bickering amongst yourselves about the style of the content, then agree a 'house style' of how the communications need to look and sound. This should make all of your communications look, feel and sound similar.
- If you find yourself pulling information together right before it needs to be sent out, then try breaking the compilation process down into small chunks and

setting reminders for yourself in your to do list software or electronic calendar so that you nibble your way through the tasks instead of leaving one massive chunk of activity until the last minute.
- If the time it takes to pull the communication together is too much, then examine the purpose of the communication and distil it down to its essence. Don't make more work for yourself than you need to. 'Spit it out' and become efficient with your words.

Regular communication is a great way to improve the business' performance. The right information in the right place at the right time can boost morale and ensure that correct decisions are made.

The communication vehicles that you select can make a big difference. Some people love the big company get together to find out about the plans for the business, some people hate it. Some people crave the focus gained from having a one-to-one discussion with their line manager and some hate it. Some prefer to receive an email whilst others prefer a hard copy document. Others get enough information from their regular business management meetings. In my experience the businesses that have a range of communication vehicles seem to do the best. The same message being transmitted via different channels has the best chance of hitting more targets. Following on from the previous section, however, don't make more work for yourself than is required. Some people don't take in any information and that will be the case regardless of how wide and engaging your channels are!

Communication is a broad area and the small section in this book will only scratch the surface. If this topic comes up in your RCA results, then finding some quick wins to improve how and what is communicated (and to whom and when) should be worth your while.

Learning

The opportunity for learning to take place after an RCA exercise is something that I always see. The reason that the issue is being investigated likely means that someone has a gap in their knowledge and that is what caused the issue.

Einstein was famously claimed to have said "the definition of insanity is doing the same thing over and over again and expecting a different result". From a root cause perspective this means that if we fail to learn something from each exercise then we have probably missed a trick somewhere along the way.

A framework that I like to run alongside the RCA process is known as 'CARL'. CARL stands for Challenge, Actions Taken, Reflection and Learning. If there are no obvious learning points from the RCA itself then the reflection and learning elements from CARL can be used to pull them out. Once you have an action plan to resolve the issue that has been through the RCA you can use the full cycle of CARL to continuously extend your learning as shown below:

Challenge: What issue you are going to resolve.
Actions Taken: The actions you took.
[Pause whilst you carry out your actions.]
Reflection: Your feelings on the results and outcomes.
Learning: What you would do differently next time.

If you are familiar with the PDCA (Plan, Do, Check, Act) cycle then you will note its similarities. I find that the different headings with CARL, however, prompt slightly different thinking and again this underpins the idea that we can take higher levels of responsibility within our businesses, become more effective and influence a positive change in the performance of the business.

Each RCA exercise is a direct learning opportunity. I hope that you find something valuable in the exercises you carry out.

Teamwork and cooperation

The majority of businesses require effective teamwork and cooperation if they are going to experience high levels of performance. It is highly likely that your RCA endeavours will uncover areas of teamwork that are lacking and this, again, is a real opportunity to improve performance.

Whereas there may be many different teams or departments at your place of work, there will still be one business (or one group). If you are embracing the idea of maximising responsibility and control, then the idea of one business will be appealing.

If you are finding that problems are being caused by other departments within your business, or that you have shortfalls in your working relationships then this is definitely an area that can be improved. I am not suggesting that you start to do all of the work for your sister departments, helping them however, because it will help you, is a reasonable strategy. Having better quality interactions with your colleagues from other departments should help overall performance and this, over time, can become the norm. I have worked in several businesses where it seemed that it was always 'take, take, take' by the other departments. When they talked issues through and started to help each other it got better. It was never perfect, although achieving higher levels of performance became easier. When resources are getting stretched it can be simpler to close the doors and focus only on your own area, but that's not a great tactic when you consider the longer-term impact on the business.

Having 'functional relationships' may be the first step on this journey. Ensuring that the right things are done at the right time, removing ego from the conversation and recognising the needs of the overall business might be enough to see a marked improvement in performance. You might never become friends with the people in the other area, but overall you can rise above this. People struggle and do all kinds of strange things when they get cornered. If we take the idea of maximising control and responsibility and apply it to working relationships, then we can move past being right about the problems and move towards achieving the results.

The ability for teams to work together and improve the overall performance and results of the business is too great to ignore.

If the topic even scrapes the surface of your conversations during your RCA, then I urge you to look a little more at it. Doing the bare minimum is fine for many businesses when it comes to relationships, but when you are looking for higher levels of performance, it has to be more than that.

Take the opportunity of improving cooperation and teamwork whenever it presents itself and see what a little bit of effort in the right area can really do!

Record keeping and filing

The ability to locate and use records in a business is often a real marker of the effectiveness of a business. I see many cases where the lack of filing and record keeping correlates with a poor general discipline around routine and day-to-day management. Quite often I will see this particular topic appear as an output of RCA exercises; failings in this area often manifest themselves as poor decision making based on poor information, a lack of joined up systems and wasting time trying to find information that you would expect to be readily available.

As a development opportunity this really is a case of 'a few seconds spent today will save hours in the future'. The requirements for good filing and record keeping are minimal; have a logical system for storing your information, know how it affects other pieces of information and do what you said you were going to do.

From a personal perspective – could you become more disciplined at filing and storing records?

From a business perspective – are your systems fit for purpose?

This development opportunity is very much around the common good of the business. The person that stores the information is not necessarily the person that is going to retrieve it later on. This is certainly an opportunity for the business to move from 'they' type discussions to 'I' type discussions. The busy-ness of day-to-day work can certainly lead you to neglect how your data and information systems work. Ensuring that they are healthy and that they can provide good management information will improve your chances of making good decisions later on (and hopefully in a quicker fashion too).

If you find an improvement opportunity around filing and

record keeping, then please don't let it pass you by. By joining up your systems you will have an opportunity to continue to learn and grow as well as to stop wasting time hunting for records in the future.

Presenting ideas and improvements

Another topic that appears on a regular basis is how effectively individuals and teams present their ideas. The clarity with which ideas are presented can make a big difference to the effectiveness of a change being implemented. Getting this right can make a big difference to the longer-term performance of a business.

A simple approach to improve the clarity of ideas is to go back to our trusted friend '5W1H'. When trying to describe an idea, or improvement activity, using the prompts of who, what, where, when, why and how can make this a whole lot easier. On many occasions the failings behind an activity will link back to a missing piece of information at the outset. These prompts, whilst not fool proof, will help to move you forward.

Being clear about the point underlying your idea / improvement is also essential. Having this crystal clear for your colleagues will help you hang the other details off it nicely. A simple structure to help with this is the point-evidence-point approach. This approach has been taught in schools and institutions for centuries and follows a simple structure. Start by making your point, back it up (ideally) with three pieces of evidence and then close with your point. This short and simple method allows for effective communication of ideas and is good for selling ideas to your colleagues.

The other point that I want to raise about presenting ideas is being clear on the cost / benefit information. Often, I will see managers trying to justify an improvement, or a position that they want to hold, and not back it up with any financial information. A simple stating of the costs involved with the activity and the potential benefits (in both monetary and other measures) can really help back up a proposal. Of course, if you haven't got numbers ready before you present your idea then it might be a case of doing some more homework before you make your proposal.

Often a good idea will be usurped by a poorer idea that is better presented. If you have found this to be the case during your RCA exercises, then I hope the tips in this section will help you to find some development opportunities for you and your team going forward.

Improving specificity

The final personal development opportunity that I see on a regular basis, via RCA, is improving specificity. In short, what is it exactly that you want from others?

I'm sure that you have seen this yourself. You ask for something to be done by another member of your team and what you get isn't what you wanted but it is what you asked for. A good step forward is to use the 5W1H headings to make sure that you cover all the bases around what it is that you want. Being more specific means knowing what is important and spelling it out.

I have been called into companies to help them out with improvement projects that had previously failed. There was nothing wrong with the improvement ideas, but the deliverables weren't specified precisely enough. For example, a company owner asked one of his teams to look into how to reduce email traffic. The team came up with alternative electronic communication methods which were rejected by the owner. He wanted them to start having face to face conversations and not send emails. He did not specify what he wanted.

Another good example is from a team that were trying to streamline one of their main business processes. They undertook an analysis of their process and shaved off approximately 15% of the work content. Not a bad result except that the director of this function wasn't happy. I was asked to have a look and, after probing the director, I found out that he required an 80% reduction in work content. The process wasn't going to be viable longer term without such a drop in activity. He never specified 80% and the vague goal given to his team was therefore ineffective. The team did reach their goal once their thinking was in the right place.

Thinking about the outcomes you want to experience and describing the important features of them to your team is required here. Like the example above, a general direction is fine as long as you don't have anywhere specific to arrive at. As I keep saying to my clients, if you want a green box then ask for a green box! I don't recall how I originally ended up talking about green boxes, but everyone knows what I mean. If you want your software solution to be able to handle high volume transactions in just three clicks, then say so. If you want your appraisal process to be re-engineered so that it takes no longer than 30 minutes to carry out, then say so. If you want your site-based teams to be able to view order information remotely via a smartphone, then say so.

You know the important outcomes you want your improvements to achieve, so spell them out.

If you find this personal development opportunity appearing via your RCA exercises, then please grab it with both hands. Being better able to specify outcomes required by your teams and their improvement projects saves a lot of time and effort in the long run.

Better meetings

Most of us get tied up in too many meetings. Saying that, I am a fan of a good, well run meeting. Many problems that I see during my client's experience of RCA involve meetings. Their complaints are often around having too many meetings and not enough time to actually do the work they should be doing. I know how they feel and I'm sure that you do too!

The link with RCA, for me, is around the ability for a meeting to produce something meaningful. That is the effectiveness of the meeting. How much time it takes and the total amount of resource it requires to achieve the output, that's the efficiency element.

If a well organised and well run meeting that produces something valuable is worthwhile, can we make them more effective and more efficient? I think that the answer is always "yes".

Planning and preparation for meetings is something that I see to be woefully inadequate in many organisations. The usual experience I see, and hear about, is that of people turning up to meetings in order to find out what the meeting is about. If people can walk into a meeting knowing what the purpose of the meeting is and know what is about to happen the meetings tend to take less time and be more productive. I'm sure that you can reflect on a great number of meetings where you waste time at the start trying to bring everyone up to speed.

How you prepare for your meetings will be largely specific to your business, but there are a few generic points to look out for.

Preparation of reports in advance helps to hold meetings 'by exception' rather than 'by everything'. If the attendees bother to review the information in advance, then this can rapidly make meetings more productive. I used the phrase 'bother to review' as this, for many, is a big cultural shift. This book is about extending personal responsibility, with enough people this is possible.

Having a standard agenda is another good way to make meetings more productive. Building on the last point, if people know what is coming, they can be prepared for it. Having the same agenda time and time again can help people get into a routine for the meetings. There is always the risk that the agenda becomes stale, but that is a small price to pay for shorter and more productive meetings. Changing a few elements of the agenda (in an agreed and controlled manner) should be all it takes to keep the meeting meaningful and valuable.

Being clear about what each attendee needs to contribute to the meetings is another good way to increase productivity. When the people attending know what is expected of them it increases commitment and buy in to the meeting format. Tying this in with the last two points; it helps with preparation and standardising the meeting. The meeting shouldn't all be down to one person to organise and 'put on a show' if it is meant to be a team effort.

When it comes down to speeding up the meetings, or put another way, getting more done in less time (aka more productive) there are few strategies I can share also.

Putting time limits onto agenda items is a really quick way to condense discussion topics. Putting a time to the slots gives the people attending a clear view of what is expected and gives them a chance to manage the level of discussion that takes place before an action is agreed upon. Getting the times right isn't always easy and if you are going down the route of a standard agenda it might take a few iterations to get this right.

Keeping on topic is another simple strategy to keep meetings short and punchy. Often people will start to discuss related items within a main topic. If you can spot this then you can nip it in the bud. It often helps to have a list of ground rules available for your meetings, that you can refer to, to make it easier to enforce.

For those topics that are taking more time than expected, you can choose to either park the conversation and reconvene (if only a fraction of the team is involved in the discussion) or alter the schedule. Some topics are important and shouldn't be rushed. Other topics should be curtailed, actions agreed, and the agenda progressed. Deciding which is which is the job of the meeting Chair and I'm sure that you will know intuitively what's what for your business.

I stand by meetings as being a force for good. They can be a nightmare, but the tips in this section should help you to streamline what you are doing currently. If meetings come up as an issue during your RCA exercises then reviewing how you conduct them is worthwhile. Even with the best intentions there is a lot of management time tied up in meetings. A good meeting can produce superb decisions and actions that can take a business forward. A bad meeting can suck away motivation and kill a diary.

How do you want your meetings to be?

Quicker decision making

Delays affect businesses in many different ways. This topic is another common one that appears at the end of RCAs. Delays often mean that people get on with something else and they don't notice the overall impact it has on the business. From processes missing their targets to deliveries going out late and frustration for all those involved, delays have a big effect.

Some of those delays are outside of your direct control. This book is all about increasing our levels of personal responsibility and control, so perhaps there is an opportunity to improve this to some degree. But there are also delays under our control that we need to look at. Many of these are linked to slow decision making on our part and this is definitely an area for improvement.

The cost of not making decisions is often under-represented. If the business needs to make a decision and it doesn't, what does that cost the business? If there are lost opportunities as a result, then there is a cash value that can be applied to the potential loss. If you have resources tied up, or working inefficiently because of the delay, then that can have a cash value. If you are able to convert the delay into a cost per hour then this recognition often helps to put decision making higher up the priority list.

The effectiveness of decisions is another related area. If the team are fearful of making a bad decision, then it is likely that the decision will be procrastinated upon. Our ability to make more effective decisions over time certainly makes everyone feel better. Monitoring, measuring, learning, documenting and sharing is the basic loop that helps decisions to become better over time. The more accurate our predictions become is directly related to our understanding of the working environment and the people within it. Learn from bad decisions and ensure that everyone grows so that better decisions can be made in the future.

Being aware of the 'point of origin' is vital here too. Being able to make decisions as close to the place and time where the decision requirement is discovered makes a massive difference. If teams under teams under teams have to wait for decisions from 'up high' for relatively small ticket items, then no wonder we have slower processes than we should. Empowering our staff to be able to make certain decisions can take this delay away and our productivity can soar. Knowing what decisions need to be made at each level and ensuring that they are trained to undertake the decision making is a good improvement opportunity. If you are unsure of what needs to be cascaded down the hierarchy, ask your supervisory staff what they are sick and tired of being asked all the time. There is a good chance that this is a clue to what decision making needs to be shared out.

On the other side of the coin there is the issue of needing support with decision making. Issues can often get stuck within the business if the decision making gets lost. This might mean that a decision doesn't get made and the team needing the decision aren't in a position to proceed. In this case a clear escalation guide could be established so that the team know how to move the issue forward if it appears to be stuck. The priority at one level for a decision to be made could be a completely different priority at another level. We all have competing demands for our time and energy and a formal escalation route allows us to navigate this situation effectively.

The results from better decision making should be obvious. Improvements happen more quickly, training gets approved / denied faster and so plans can be made, projects don't get stuck for as long and morale improves. Not everything will be in your control to change with regards to delays, but there is always something you can do. If delays and decision making appears in your RCA exercises then review the scopes of control and decision making and see if you can improve things a little for the whole business.

Better use of KPIs

My final generic RCA output to consider is Key Performance Indicators (KPIs). This topic usually appears indirectly and is another good area to review when looking for business wide improvements. Again, there are benefits to both the business and individual with this item. The reason that it keeps on popping up as a topic is that formally monitoring and measuring the performance of a business is something that often gets missed when the day to day workload gets too much. If it doesn't get missed out altogether then it can often become sporadic, which doesn't support your ongoing management and decision-making activities.

Keeping score is a vital business task. Being able to measure the right things at the right time is a key skill when leading and managing a business. So, let me give you this challenge; are you measuring the right things in your business? If you take your existing performance measures, do they help you to run your business? It is very easy to take a handful of measures and not find out anything about what is really going on, you just have a series of numbers, percentages and pretty graphs. If you don't feel that you have the right KPIs to drive the right behaviours and performance in your business, then it is worth taking another look.

Taking responsibility when it comes to KPIs leads us to look at moving from just recording the data to using it as information. I walk into lots of offices and see charts, tables and graphs adorning the walls. After a little bit of questioning I often find out that they are simply decorations. The questions that I ask around how teams use the data are often met with blank stares. I have two simple tests for KPIs; can they be used to make decisions and are they being used? The first point is simple enough, if they can't be used then they need to be changed. The second point harks back to the theme of personal responsibility and a decision to use the information is purely down to us.

Good KPIs should help to drive the right behaviours in the business. If they are not having the right impact (or any impact at all) then they become candidates for change. This point, of course, ties in with the last point. If there is no follow up, no accountability associated with the results then we need to start there. When this is in place the KPIs should help motivate the team to perform in the correct manner. I recall a factory that measured pieces produced and paid a large proportion of their staff accordingly. Guess what? These people produced whatever they could fastest and not necessarily what the business needed to satisfy the customer's demands. It wasn't until we moved to a profit share approach (for the entire business) that we could change the behaviour of this portion of the employees.

Going back to our personal responsibility for a moment, the purpose of KPIs is to inform our thinking so that we can take the business 'onwards and upwards'. If your current suite of KPIs aren't making the grade, then this is your opportunity to look at changing them. Hopefully you have the authority to do this in your business, otherwise it is your responsibility to start negotiating! Don't put up with useless measures. Define some simple and practical measures that, when read together, tell you how things are really going. From here you can develop a routine to review the measures and develop improvement action plans that will take you to where you need to go.

In business we need results, results and results! KPIs are a great tool to help direct our energies and focus. Whether or not your RCA exercises throw out KPIs as a topic, take this opportunity to grab them and make them what you need them to be.

This concludes my thoughts on the opportunities that often show their head after conducting an RCA exercise. I hope that the topics have given you something to think about. The whole point of finding the root cause is to find a fundamental issue within your business that you can resolve. By nature, being at cause means that the change is in your control. A few basic changes can have a huge outcome. I have seen what happens when you do this for my clients, and I have seen it in my own career.

Also, don't underestimate the personal development angle presented here. If you change for the better, then everything else does too. If you get just a little bit better, this will amplify through every other activity you touch. For me, the personal development activity is primary to the business improvements. If you can improve then you will take the business with you.

Let's move on to the conclusion of this book and I'll share with you my closing remarks.

Conclusion

Now that you have reached the end of this book, how do you feel?

Do you think that making a few tweaks to how you carry out a root cause analysis will make a difference to how your business performs? I hope so.

When I have been impressed with the scale of a business' improvement, it has never been a big thing that has made the difference. It has been a small thing (or a handful of small things). There have been a few instances over the last ten years that have stood out to me:

- The senior manager that realised that how they asked their questions affected the outcome. They tweaked their style and unlocked the potential of their team.
- The team that realised that saying 'that's not good enough' (in a nice way) was the only way that they were going to raise standards and then watched as they quickly did.
- The business that grasped that spelling out clearly what they wanted to experience shouldn't be taken for granted. We then watched their staff flourish under the

clear direction as the business performed beyond expectations.

Pushing an RCA to the level of these microscopic personal changes might take a bit more effort in an already stretched diary, but the outcomes are worth it. To round off this book, I will now summarise the key points of this book.

This can be a big ask

To go back to the 'warning' at the start of this book, this approach isn't for everyone. I think that it should be, but it can be a bitter pill to swallow. If this approach excites you as to what the results could be longer term that is great. Realise that other people in your business might not be as excited initially about the prospect of pointing the finger back at themselves.

Over time this should become easier if others in your organisation take the lead. Like raising non-conformance reports, it only gets easier after there has been a volume experienced beforehand. The potential for making small improvements over a wide area of activity, all centred around taking more responsibility, is huge. If you think this is going to be a big ask for your teams then show them how it can be done.

This applies everywhere

The idea of properly applying RCA applies everywhere. It isn't just limited to business, but that is the focus for this book. Many organisations seem to apply RCA effectively in very specific areas (such as incident investigation and production mistakes) but they stop there.

You have the opportunity to apply RCA to every area of your business and see what learning comes out from it. Not only should you be solving problems that have plagued your business, your teams should improve too. If each RCA fixed a problem with your operations and your team found a nugget of truth that they could embrace about their own performance just imagine where you would be in a year from now.

Don't limit the ideas from this book to just one area of your business. By all means start small but expand until every area is constructively critical of the problems it encounters. Egos need to be put back in their boxes, for sure, but the results are worth the short-term pain.

Control is available at every level

Every person that touches the issue / process that you review has some degree of control. Whether this is full control at the higher levels of the organisation, or a comparatively small level of control at the lower levels, there is something. Exercising this control has been the underpinning message of this book and reinforcing it in your business will bring you results.

Don't pass by this opportunity. Share with your teams the ideas from this book and let them embrace their control. Whether this is as simple as people flagging up things that aren't right in the business or as personal as realising shortcomings (and their corresponding development opportunities), there will be something that you can do.

Having an open conversation about personal shortcomings is a very mature conversation. Again, it is not for everyone but, if you get a few people of influence in your business on-board, magical things can start to happen. This, once more, is an opportunity for you to lead by example.

Maximum responsibility equals maximum productivity

What is the payoff for extending RCA down to a very personal level?

If everyone in our organisation was reflective and embraced the full responsibilities that they had, we would be able to maximise our productivity. This is a fairly utopian view but is something that we can strive for.

From my experience this idea will only be grasped by a small handful of senior business leaders in any organisation and a handful of their 'up and coming' star players. Most people will not embrace the full extent of a root cause analysis in the way that I have described it in this book.

This is OK. Not everyone will go for every idea. Not every person will be onboard with all of your changes. That's life. Thankfully you don't need everyone onboard to witness some really profound changes and results to make it worthwhile.

Start with yourself and see what results you get. Once you're happy, extend the ideas to your team and see what happens. Once you're happy with this, extend the ideas up and down the organisation (depending on where you are situated of course). Take it steady and remember that this kind of continuous improvement will not be everyone's cup of tea (so to speak!).

If we want to experience the best results and outcomes for our business, then there needs to be high levels of responsibility coupled with great processes and systems. This extension of RCA could help you move closer to the organisation you want to run.

Thank you for joining me on this short journey to look at a twist on an already very effective business improvement tool. I wish you all the best with the onward part of your journey.

Giles

Reference and further reading

"Do you want to be right, or do you want results?"

Dennis Stevenson

Strachar E & Stevenson D, 'Creating Financial Flow with Dennis Stevenson', on Into the Genius Zone, Audio Book, In Genius Inc, USA

On Time Delivery – A Real Lean Manufacturing Story

Read about my journey to transform an underperforming manufacturing operation and the lessons learned.

Available in paperback and for electronic reader.

https://www.amazon.co.uk/dp/1973201747

https://www.smashwords.com/books/view/302166

https://itunes.apple.com/gb/book/on-time-delivery-real-lean/id631538971?mt=11

Making It Happen (online course)

Join my online programme and discover a great range of practical and highly effective business improvement and change management strategies. Get the first month free!

https://making-it-happen.dpdcart.com/subscriber/signup

About Giles

Giles is a Chartered Engineer with a background in Production Engineering and Operations Management. He spends most of his time working on Lean, ERP and Operations Management improvement projects.

Giles has worked in a variety of different roles within manufacturing prior to working as a consultant for a prestigious university.

In 2005 Giles decided to forge his own path and created Smartspeed, which has been helping businesses to improve their delivery performance and productivity levels, along with their profits, ever since.

Giles can be contacted by:
Email -   gilesjohnston@smartspeed.co.uk
Website -   www.smartspeed.co.uk

Printed in Great Britain
by Amazon